The Walking Dunes:
East Hampton's Hidden Treasure

CORRECTIONS TO 1ST EDITION

Pages 18-19: According to Suffolk County
entomologist Dr. Scott Campbell, what many
hikers on eastern Long Island assumed were
Chiggers (*Trombicula alfreddugesi*), and gave
them a chiggers-like rash, were in fact Lone Star
Tick larvae (*Amblyomma americanum*). No
Chiggers have been documented in Suffolk
County.

Page 58: The picture mislabeled Scotch Broom
is Cypress Spurge (*Eurphoriba cyparissias*), in
the spurge family.

Page 99: The common names for *Rosa Rugosa*
are Rugosa Rose or Beach Rose.

Page 101: The genus for *Gerardia* is now
Agalinis.

Page 102: The unlabeled photo on the left is
Canada Toadflax (*Nuttallanthus canadensis*).

*NOTE: Thanks to Stephen Young, Chief
Botanist with the New York Natural Heritage
Program, for providing these corrections.*

The Walking Dunes:
East Hampton's Hidden Treasure

Photographs by Ruth Formanek

Text by Mike Bottini

Pogonia Books

Table Of Contents

Ruth's Acknowledgements

Many friends, colleagues and relatives helped this book along. I thank Mike Bottini for being a most knowledgable and inquisitive naturalist, and exceptional writer. Estelle Gellman was my gracious host after I moved to New York City and needed bed and board during my visits to the Walking Dunes. Anita Gurian, my co-author on previous books, served as enthusiastic editor and consultant. My granddaughter Martina Mansell was the talented copy editor and proof reader. I am grateful for the contributions of a critical audience, which every photographer craves: Athan and Margot Karras, Paul Stetzer, Margery Franklin, Helen and Chuck Pine, Nancy Sirkis, Elsa Blum, Myron Brenton, David Formanek, Miriam Forman-Brunell, Andrew Gurian, Gisa Indenbaum, Judy Rosenblatt, June Zaccone, the Park West Camera Club, and Soho Photo Gallery, where some of my prints were exhibited. I thank my grandchildren Perry and Zoe Brunell, the East Hampton Trails Preservation Society and the many friends who went hiking into the Dunes with me. On one trip Perry found the tiny insectivorous Sundews for me. I had read Ann F. Johnson's *Guide to the Plant Communities of the Napeague Dunes* (1985, unfortunately out of print), and was delighted when Ann agreed to write the Preface.

But can one thank software programs? In this case, yes. In addition to Adobe Photoshop CS3, I want to express my admiration of and gratitude to Adobe InDesign CS3 which permitted me to do a first draft of the manuscript's layout by myself. Naomi Rosenblatt, a gifted book designer, then gave shape to the book as well as lots of valuable technical advice.

Many people have asked how Mike Bottini and I came to collaborate on a book. I had thought about a book of Dunes photographs after I had been shooting them for many, many years. In 2003, I read in Mike's *Trail Guide to the South Fork* that the Walking Dunes were his "…favorite area for nature interpretation—that is, figuring out why certain plants are growing where they are and what the area might look like in the near future." I contacted him, invited him to view some of my Dunes photos (which at the time were in a local show) and he agreed to write the text for this book.

Mike's Acknowledgements

I was first introduced to the Walking Dunes area by Laura Newgard, a colleague at the environmental advocacy organization called Group for the South Fork (now Group for the East End) in the spring of 1988. That June I joined John Turner and Eric Lamont on a Long Island Botanical Society survey of orchids on eastern Long Island, a long day in the field that ended at the Walking Dunes cranberry bog. I learned much about the area and natural history in general from both over the years since.

During the summer of 1988 I found myself leading guided hikes through the area for New York State Parks Superintendent George Larson, who encouraged me to develop interpretive material and a marked nature trail there. This was eventually implemented under the tenure of Superintendent Tom Dess, George's replacement upon his retirement from State Parks.

Professor Larry McCormick of Southampton College was kind enough to permit me to tag along on his geology field trips to the Walking Dunes. He and Professor John Black of Suffolk Community College were both very helpful in explaining the physical processes that create and maintain dunes in general, as well as offering their thoughts on the origin of the Walking Dunes in particular. Cynthia Dietz, the map librarian at Stony Brook University, was a great help in locating maps of eastern Long Island from the 1800s.

Irwin Brodo, Jean Held, and Lance Biechele answered lots of questions about lichens and fungi. Lance identified the mysterious asphalt-like organism* that is ubiquitous among the dunes of Napeague and that stumped me, as well as every other naturalist I showed it to, for many years.

Finally, although I have never met Ann Johnson, her excellent book, *Plant Communities of the Napeague Dunes*, accompanied me on most of my visits to the Walking Dunes.

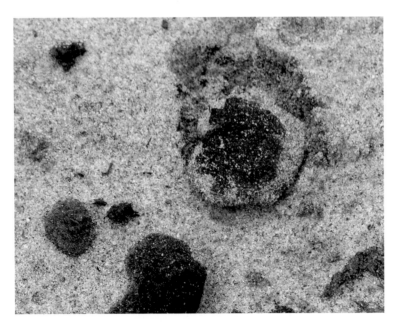

Tar Spot Lichen. See Lichen Chapter.

'Landscape in Motion'

Preface by Ann F. Johnson, Ph.D.*

The Walking Dunes of Hither Hills State Park have a story to tell and here is the perfect book to help you decipher it. This is a landscape in motion, shaped by the same forces that shaped the rest of Long Island: ice, waves and, in this case most particularly, wind. First the ice of the glacial conveyor belt scraped rocks, sand, and silt off the surface of New England and carried them southward to the line where it melted back as fast as it advanced, depositing them in a jumbled pile on the continental shelf to form Long Island. Then ocean waves eroded the edges of this jumbled mass, leaving the heavier rocks behind to fall in place, keeping the finer silts in suspension to settle in quiet water farther out to sea, and moving the sand along the shore to build the beaches and fill in gaps in the line of glacial deposits. Finally the wind blew the sand off the beach and piled it up against the first obstacle it met. In the normal course of events that obstacle would be beach grass whose underground stems grow upward as they are buried to build the familiar dunes that parallel the shore. How the sand got away from the stabilizing beach grass and began to move inland engulfing whole forests forms the story of the Walking Dunes told here.

From the sweeping panorama at the crest of the dunes to the Lilliputian cranberry bogs at their base, Ruth Formanek and Mike Bottini closely intertwine pictures and words to give us both an overview of the world of the Walking Dunes and close-up views of its inhabitants and how they survive there. The book begins where the trail does, at the edge of a forest rooted in the path of the North Dune, a slowly advancing tsunami of sand. The first plant introduced, for very practical reasons, is Poison Ivy. The photograph shows its leaves fairly gleaming with menace, but we learn from the text that it is not only the leaves we need to be able to recognize, and so go back to give all its parts a careful look! From the forest we skirt the base of the current Walking Dune and meet the hardy pioneers that manage to surf the sand wave itself, beach grass, beach heather, and bearberry. Along the crest we walk over the tops of buried trees, gazing south across the canopies of those yet to be buried at the crests of the Middle and oldest Walking Dunes in the distance, mute evidence that what is happening now has happened before and will perhaps one day happen again. Descending into the bowl of the North Dune we come to the damp flats left in its wake, now covered by cranberries, orchids, and sphagnum moss.

View down from the North Dune toward Napeague Harbor. Springs peninsula in the background.

The shimmering beauty of the Grass Pink orchid captured in close-up takes on new overtones when we learn how it is used: to tempt young bees into making fools of themselves, not just once but at least twice! And so, dear reader, I wish you happy trails, both armchair and actual, reading the story of "The Walking Dunes."

Grass Pink, a wild Orchid

Rose pogonia, a wild Orchid

*Ann F. Johnson, Ph.D., is the author of *A Guide to the Plant Communities of the Napeague Dunes (1985)*. She is currently Community Ecologist with Florida Natural Areas Inventory, Tallahassee, Florida.

Introduction

This book of photographs and explanatory text represents our invitation to nature lovers--hikers, photographers, children, adults and seniors alike--to discover the particular beauty of this unusual landscape: the picturesque dune formations which "walked" over forest and marsh, burying trees, shrubs and other vegetation. We want to share our love of the unique Walking Dunes of eastern Long Island.

Directions to the Walking Dunes

Coming from the west on Montauk Highway (Route 27), continue approximately six miles east of the center of Amagansett, and turn left onto Napeague Harbor Road. Cross the LIRR tracks, and continue 0.25 mile to the junction of the Paumanok Path (marked with white rectangular trail blazes) or 1.5 miles to where the road ends on Napeague Harbor, and the Walking Dunes Nature Trail begins. At either location, find a suitable place to park on the road shoulder.

Cautions for Visitors

As with other nature preserves on eastern Long Island, be aware of Ticks, Chiggers, and Poison Ivy. Stay on the marked trails and avoid brushing against trailside vegetation.

Trail Access

Two trails provide access to the Walking Dunes area: the **Walking Dunes Nature Trail** and the **Paumanok Path**. The mile-long **Walking Dunes Nature Trail** begins at the north end of Napeague Harbor Road and loops through a portion of the most active of the three parabolic (U-shaped) dunes, the North Dune. It's the most easily accessed and frequently visited area of the Walking Dunes.

The Nature Trail was established in 1990 at the urging of Hither Hills Park Superintendent George Larson, who had noted increased damage to the area. The footsteps of visitors, including naturalists, school groups and photographers, as well as ORVs (off-road vehicles) had

View from the Walking Dunes Nature Trail

created several blowouts in the area. Today, ORVs are restricted to the shoreline of Napeague Harbor, and visitors are asked to stay off steep slopes and walk on the designated trails to limit foot-traffic impact.

The Trail was designed in consultation with local naturalists, botanists and teachers who led trips to the area. The trail encompasses most of the diverse features of the Walking Dunes, including the cranberry bog with rare orchids and carnivorous plants, a freshwater wetland that is in the process of being covered by the advancing dune sand, and an amazing view of the parabolic dune from the dune crest. Several modifications to the trail have been made since 1990, and will continue to be made in the future, reflecting the dynamic nature of this area.

The **Paumanok Path** (white rectangular blazes) crosses Napeague Harbor Road a quarter-mile north of the LIRR (Long Island Rail Road) tracks, and heads easterly onto the oldest and most stable of the three parabolic dunes, the South Dune. The Paumanok Path is a regional trail that currently extends the entire length of East Hampton Town, a distance of 45 miles from the Montauk lighthouse west into Southampton. Look for Prickly Pear cactus near the trail not far in from the road. This trail climbs a steep embankment of glacial deposits upon which the South Dune sits and traverses a relatively flat hilltop where Pink Lady's Slipper orchids can be found. The Paumanok Trail also provides an interesting view of the highest point of the Middle Dune where the trail exits the Walking Dunes area, a distance of 0.7 mile from Napeague Harbor Road.

Small Black Cherry trees, an early successional or pioneer species, begin the process of reclaiming a former forest area that was smothered by the South Dune, seen in the background.

Before You Go: Recognize Poison Ivy!

Because it can inflict a severe rash, Poison Ivy (*Toxicodendron radicans* or *Rhus radicans*) is an important plant to recognize. Look for it along the first fifty feet of the Walking Dunes Nature Trail, near its starting point at the end of Napeague Harbor Road.

The ubiquitous Poison Ivy thrives in a wide variety of soil and sunlight conditions. As testament to its adaptability and hardiness, it can be found in all Napeague's plant communities except the lower salt marsh. It also grows in a variety of forms and sizes, a characteristic that fools many naturalists. Tree-like specimens can be found on the Isle of Shoals off the coast of New Hampshire. A vine in nearby Camp Hero State Park is as thick as an arm and reaches fifty feet into the forest canopy!

Whether a small tree, low shrub, or vine, all parts of the plant (roots, leaves, berries and stems) contain the poisonous oil, a phenol called urushiol, at all times of the year. Therefore, one should learn to identify Poison Ivy with and without its leaves.

Identification is not as simple as many naturalists would have you believe. One reliable identifying feature is its compound leaf comprised of three leaflets. Although there are many other plants with three leaflets, the adage "Leaflets three, let it be!" is worth keeping in mind.

Many references state that Poison Ivy's leaves are a very shiny green, and a few claim that its leaflet edges are smooth, not toothed or serrated as in the business edge of a saw. Unfortunately, there are enough exceptions to both, seen in dull green leaves and clearly toothed leaflets, particularly the latter, that these characteristics are not reliable.

The fall foliage of Poison Ivy varies along a spectrum from pale yellow to a brilliant scarlet-red (not unlike that of Virginia Creeper), and when they first emerge in spring, the tiny leaves are a distinctive pale-red (not unlike the color of new oak leaves). During the leafless months between, their presence is marked by its small, whitish berries (technically these are drupes) that often persist well into winter (careful, they somewhat resemble Bayberry) and hair-like, aerial rootlets. The problem is, plants that grow in shade often do not flower and produce berries (they spread via underground rhizomes). And specimens that are not climbing up other plants do not always produce aerial roots. Even experienced naturalists can mistakenly wander into a large patch of berry-less, leaf-less, calf-high Poison Ivy shrubs in winter.

Some people are so susceptible to Poison Ivy that they claim they can contract the rash merely by walking near a plant. In fact, not only must contact be made with part of the plant, but that part of the plant must have the oil on its surface, which only happens if the plant has been damaged. Keep in mind, though, that insect activity, animal browse, and even the wind can cause enough damage to expose the oil.

We are all immune to Poison Ivy at birth. At estimated 15% of the population maintains immunity for life; the rest of us develop reactions only after several exposures to the oil.

The urushiol oil is amazingly potent. A nanogram (that's one billionth of a gram) of the oil is enough to cause a rash. To put that in some perspective, the amount of oil that can fit on the head of a pin is enough to infect 500 people, and a quarter ounce (by weight) of the stuff can give a rash to everyone in the world. So if you think you can count on seeing traces of the oil on the plant or yourself, forget about it.

The oil also has amazing longevity. There have been cases of botanists contracting a rash after handling dried herbarium specimens that were 100 years old! This poses a challenge for people in the field who regularly get the oil on their tools and boots.

In regard to spreading the oil (and rash), the rash blisters are composed of body fluids, not urushiol. Blister fluid does not spread the rash. Many people mistakenly associate a spreading rash with the release of the fluid from scratching broken blisters; the culprit, however, is usually the oil trapped beneath fingernails that is spread by scratching, with the rashes taking the form of long, thin lines. The skin on the palms of our hands and soles of our feet is too thick for the oil to penetrate and cause a rash.

If you realize that you've been in contact with Poison Ivy, rinse the exposed skin with water as soon as possible, then wash with soap and rinse thoroughly. Be sure to scrub beneath your fingernails. Toss your

field clothes in the wash, and stay out of the hot tub. Topical corticosteroids are helpful for relieving the itch.

There are some who claim you can redevelop immunity by eating the young leaves of Poison Ivy. Others claim that doing so is likely to result in a visit to the emergency room, so it's obviously not recommended.

Another situation that can send you to the emergency room is inhaling smoke from burning Poison Ivy plants. Fire releases urushiol into the air and, if inhaled, can wreak havoc on your respiratory system.

By the way, humans and a few other species of higher primates are the only animals that develop the reaction to urushiol. Over 60 species of birds feed on the berries, several mammals browse its twigs, and your pets can roll around in the stuff with no worries. That is, until they jump in your lap!

Deer Tick

American Dog Tick

Lone Star Tick

Photos by R.Gadd @
tickinfo.com

Before You Go: Ticks and Chiggers!

Three species of ticks and one mite that parasitize humans can be encountered in the Walking Dunes area: the Dog Tick *(Dermacentor variabilis)*, the Deer or Black-legged Tick *(Ixodes scapularis)*, the Lone Star Tick *(Amblyomma americanum)* and the mite, Chigger *(Trombicula alfreddugesi)*. All four species have four distinct life stages: egg, larval, nymph and adult. The larvae of each are six-legged; nymphs and adults have eight legs.

Ticks

Once they hatch, ticks require a blood meal in order to molt and progress to the next life stage. Adult females also require a blood meal in order to produce eggs. The adult males mate with feeding adult females while the females are parasitizing their final host, and males may feed periodically for short intervals during that time. During the feedings the ticks may contract one or more types of bacteria or protozoa from an infected host and transmit diseases to future hosts during subsequent feedings. Tick-transmitted diseases include Lyme Disease, Rocky Mountain Spotted Fever, Ehrlichiosis, and Babesia, among others.

These ticks only feed three times during their approximately two-year life spans, and they can survive up to a year between feedings, provided they have access to a humid environment (e.g., the moist microhabitat found in leaf litter on the forest floor). Despite several water conservation adaptations, dehydration from hot, dry weather combined with no access to mulch can be fatal to ticks (NOTE: put clothing in the dryer when returning from a tick-infested field trip).

Large portions of the Walking Dunes have no leaf litter or mulch and can be safely explored without picking up ticks.

As a general rule, ticks looking for a blood meal lie in wait on the tips of grasses, leaves and low plants for a passing host, and are most often picked up by humans on the legs below the knees. Because of this, staying on well-worn trails and avoiding contact with low vegetation greatly reduces the chance of encountering ticks.

Once a tick climbs aboard, it moves upward in search of skin and a suitable place to feed. Therefore, tucking pant legs into socks made of a tight weave prevents ticks from making contact with skin and, in combination with a tick repellent, provides an effective barrier for ticks. The best tick repellents contain a chemical called permethrin, which should be applied to pants, socks and boots (when not being worn) and allowed to dry. The treatment lasts for several months and is effective even after several trips through the washing machine.

Since they have not had a blood meal, the tiny, hard-to-see, larval ticks cannot transmit disease. But the bites of Lone Star Tick larvae have been found to mimic the agonizing itch and rash of Chiggers' bites. The population of Lone Star Ticks seems to have risen dramatically in recent years. One study reported a 3:1 ratio of Lone Star Ticks to Deer Ticks on the South Fork of Long Island and Fire Island. To avoid Lone Star Tick larvae and Chiggers, take the same precautions mentioned above.

Chiggers

Chiggers or Red Bugs *(Trombicula alfreddugesi)* are parasitic only during their larval stage. As nymphs and adults, these eight-legged creatures prey on springtails and other small organisms and their eggs that live in the soil. As with tick larvae, mite larvae have six legs. They are orange-yellow-light-red colored, and 1/120th inch in diameter (one-third the size of Lone Star Tick larvae).

Unlike ticks, Chiggers do not feed on blood. They inject an enzyme that liquefies skin cells and causes the adjacent area to harden, resulting in the formation of a straw-like tube through which they suck up and feed on partially digested skin cells. If not disturbed, feeding continues for four days. Apparently this never happens on human hosts because Chiggers have very soft mouth parts, and welts and severe itching develop soon after the bite. Scratching easily dislodges them from their feeding tubes. In fact, feeding Chiggers are easily brushed off by rubbing with a hand or a cloth. This damages their mouth parts so they are unable to resume feeding, and they perish. The feeding tube remains, however, and unfortunately is the source of the horrible itch. Intense itching can persist for ten days or longer.

Chiggers are inactive in temperatures below 60°F, and remain dormant in the soil through the winter months. Ticks, on the other hand, can be encountered on any mild day throughout the year. Unlike chiggers, do not rely on simply brushing or showering to remove ticks from your skin.

Red Maple trees partially covered by the dune.

Chigger larva, magnified from its actual microscopic size. (rendered by Naomi Rosenblatt)

Part I: Meet the Walking Dunes

The Walking Dunes encompass an area of 500 acres on the western edge of Hither Hills State Park, a 1,700 acre park spanning from ocean to bay and established in 1924 by State Park Commissioner Robert Moses. The Walking Dunes are bordered on the north by Napeague Bay, the west by Napeague Harbor, the south by the Long Island Rail Road (LIRR) and Montauk Highway (Rte. 27), and the east by Fresh Pond and the Hither Hills Park forest.

In addition to the linear dunes that typically front Long Island's ocean, bays, and harbors, the Walking Dunes area contains three U-shaped or parabolic dunes inland of the linear dunes. Under certain conditions, linear dunes may be transformed into parabolic dunes. Storm winds may provide the initial disturbance that creates a blowout in the linear dune, and strong winds move and shape it into the parabolic form (looking down from above) for which it is named. The parabolic shape is enhanced by vegetation that slows down and may anchor its ends to create long, trailing ridges of sand as it migrates downwind.

Three parabolic dunes have formed and migrated in a southeasterly direction, driven by northwesterly winds blowing across Gardiners and Napeague Bays. Although this region's prevailing winds are south-westerly, its strongest winds are from the northwest quadrant.

Top of North Dune's parabola. According to popular legend, Rudolph Valentino's film, The Sheik, *was filmed in these Sahara-like sands.*

It has been suggested that the northwest wind speeds are amplified here by the alignment of two land masses, Gardiners Island and the Springs peninsula (see map on page 24), in such as a way as to create a wind funnel (Black, 1993). This theory, however, has not been tested with wind instruments. The movement of these parabolic dunes, notably that of the North Dune, has given rise to their name, "The Walking Dunes."

View southeasterly from inside the North Dune towards its somewhat stabilized south flank (center) and actively moving apex (left).

The Origin of the Walking Dunes

Several theories on the origin and development of the Walking Dunes have been offered, but a definitive explanation of all aspects of these curious landforms remains elusive. The earliest published reference to at least one of the Walking Dunes is found in a book by geologist Myron Fuller. Fuller points out that the high elevation (100 feet) of the dune east of Napeague Harbor might be due in part to its position over elevated glacial material, a fact overlooked by several later researchers and authors. Fuller continues: "The dunes of Napeague Beach [linear coastal dunes] have derived their materials mainly from shore wash from the east; those east of Napeague Harbor [the Walking Dunes] seem to have been supplied mainly from the same source with relatively little additions from the north side, their accumulation taking place mainly under the action of the southwest winds" (Fuller, 1914). Regarding the source of sands for the Walking Dunes, all other published material is in disagreement.

Surprisingly, botanist Norman Taylor makes no mention of the Walking Dunes in his otherwise comprehensive botanical survey of Montauk (Taylor, 1923). The first detailed research and published account of the Walking Dunes was undertaken in the late 1970s by another botanist — Ann Johnson.

Johnson writes that the Walking Dunes may have been created by the activities of three menhaden fish-processing factories, the first built in 1858 that operated on the east shore of Napeague Harbor. She lists road building, woodcutting, and the sinking of wells as potential disturbances to the plant cover that set the dune sands in motion.

Remnants of the Hicks Island fish factory.

23

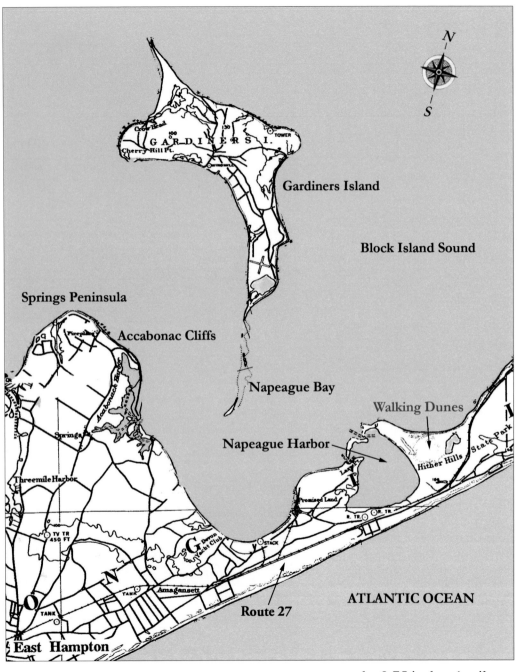

This map shows the region surrounding the Walking Dunes, including the Springs peninsula, Napeague, Napeague Harbor, parts of Hither Hills State Park with the Walking Dunes, and Gardiners Island. Montauk is to the right and Amagansett and East Hampton are to the left.

scale: 0.75 inch = 1 mile

This illustration, entitled Factory at Napeague, N.Y., first appeared in George Brown Goode's book on the American Menhaden, in 1877. (The print is available from the University of Washington Digital Collections, Plate No. 26.)

The activities of the fish-processing factories, including wood cutting and the sinking of wells, may have disturbed the existing plant cover and set the dune sands in motion, thus helping to create the Walking Dunes.

As evidence, Johnson presents two U. S. Coast Survey maps: one dated 1845 (pre-dating the factories) and another dated 1892 that shows the location of the three factories. Johnson's redrawn 1845 map is interpreted as bearing no evidence of any parabolic dunes, while the 1892 map clearly shows a parabolic dune positioned landward of a linear coastal dune and halfway between the tip of Goff Point and Montauk Highway. The 1892 map also shows a significant decrease in the amount of forest cover in the Walking Dunes area, perhaps reflecting clearing activities associated with the fish factories. This loss of forest cover is not direct evidence that the coastal dunes were destabilized, but the transport of wood from upland areas, and the unloading of fish and supplies from shore to the factory sites, most likely destroyed dune vegetation.

Johnson's hypothesis may be correct in explaining the origin of two of the three Walking Dunes, the Middle and North Dunes, but the maps themselves contain evidence that the South Dune formed prior to the establishment of the fish factories.

The map that Johnson redrew and labeled "1845" in her book more closely resembles the U.S. Coast Survey map (drawn by surveyors Renard and Sands) dated 1838. On that 1838 map, the area now covered by the South Dune is depicted as a tree-less area with significant topographic relief somewhat in the shape of a parabola. Unfortunately, these early coastal survey maps lack the topographic detail of today's maps and are difficult to interpret accurately. It is not clear whether

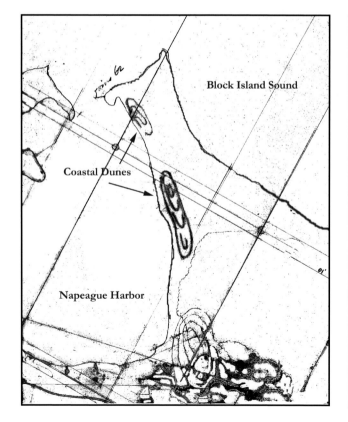

1838

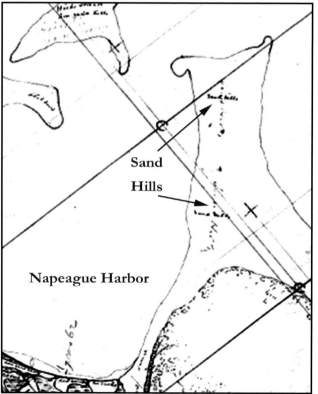

1845

this feature is composed of glacial till, dune sands, or a combination of both.

However, the 1845 U. S. Coast Survey map (surveyed by W. W. Boyce) more clearly depicts a parabolic landform in this same area. This map includes an interesting handwritten note over the area where the South Dune sits today: "sand hills." This map provides evidence that at least one of the three Walking Dunes, the South Dune, predates the construction of the fish factories. And since the area to the north and west of this dune, presumably the area that was at one time in the wake of the moving parabolic dune, is shown as being completely forested on the 1845 map, the dune itself must have formed and moved to that location many years prior to 1845.

In **summary**, the origins of the Middle and the North Dunes can be traced to the period between 1845 and 1892. The South Dune was formed some time before 1845. A map dated 1904 shows all three Walking Dunes, with the South and Middle Dunes having a shape and location very similar to that found one hundred years later.

In regard to the sources of sand for the Walking Dunes, most researchers agree that the sources are the eroding bluffs located to the west (Accabonac Cliffs) and east (Hither Woods) of Napeague Harbor. Littoral currents (currents close to the shore) move the sand along the bay shore and deposit it to form spits, sublittoral sand bars and tidal deltas near Lazy Point, Hicks Island and Goff Point (Sirkin, 1995; Black, 1993; Davis and Cangelosi, 2005).

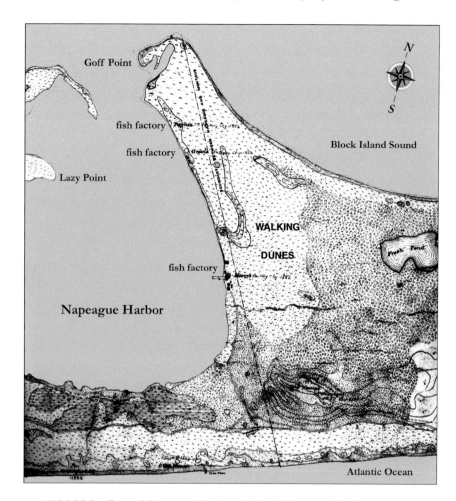

1892 U.S. Coastal Survey with sites of three Napeague Fish Factories

Aerial photographs and recent field observations show that the sand deposited on the Hicks Island spit (at the east inlet), the Goff Point spit, and the east inlet's flood tidal delta combine to form an extensive sand flat. This sand flat may eventually extend eastward into the deep (10 ft) channel that parallels the harbor's east shore and reach the northeast shore of Napeague Harbor, replenishing the beach there. Wind transport of the sand off the beach and onto the linear coastal dune, where it is trapped by beachgrass and other dune vegetation, causes the dune to grow in height and girth.

It appears that the sand spit - delta feature, or the offshore sand ridge (Black, 1993), will intersect the east shore of Napeague Harbor at a very narrow point, thereby providing sand nourishment to a very limited stretch of beach. This point is located just south of the wetland feature named Skunk's Hole, and correlates with the highest point (20.5 ft above mean sea level, or amsl) in a linear dune system whose average height ranges between 7 and 8 ft amsl (SCDPW Five Town Topo Map, 1972).

There is some speculation that, as this twenty foot-tall and 300 foot-long section of linear dune is fed by sand deposits and continues to grow, it will reach a size and height that will cause it to become unstable under the influence of the northwest wind. These dune sands will then re-form as a blowout, or parabolic, dune (Black, 1993).

The east inlet had not been dredged until the winter of 2007. The mechanisms of (1) sand transport, from bayside bluffs to inlet shoals to beach deposits via littoral currents, and (2) beach deposits to linear dunes to parabolic dunes via wind, raise another question: What impact will inlet dredging and maintenance have on the development of future Walking Dunes?

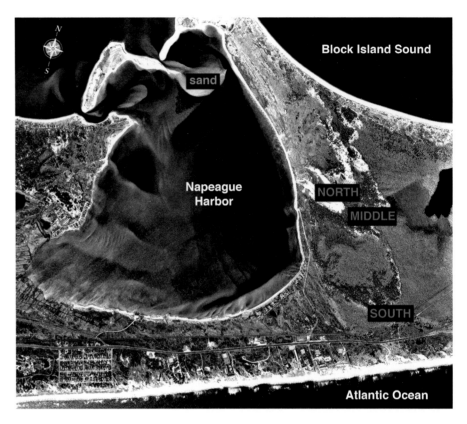

This aerial photo of Napeague Harbor, taken in 2000, shows North, South and Middle Dunes, and the large Sand Flat at the east inlet.

The Dunes Described

All three dunes (South, Middle, North) are connected by way of a sandy ridge that forms their eastern flank, and all three have the general parabolic (U) shape for which they are named. However, a close look at the topographic map reveals three general differences among the parabolic dunes: overall size, complexity of each dune's outline, and maximum elevation.

The outline of the North Dune can fit neatly inside the Middle Dune, which in turn could nestle inside the U-shape of the South Dune, like a set of slightly different-sized horseshoes. And the neatness of each dune's parabolic shape deteriorates markedly from the South Dune to the North Dune, with the latter's topographic outline tracing a series of smaller sub-parabolas. Some researchers have subdivided the North Dune into three smaller, distinct but interconnected parabolic dunes (labeled 1, 2, 3, on the topographic map).

The South Dune, in addition to being the widest of the three, is also the highest in elevation. The most recent detailed topographic map for the area lists maximum elevations as 90 ft amsl for the South Dune, 56 ft for the Middle Dune, and 42 ft for the North Dune (SCDPW Five Towns Topographic Map, 1972).

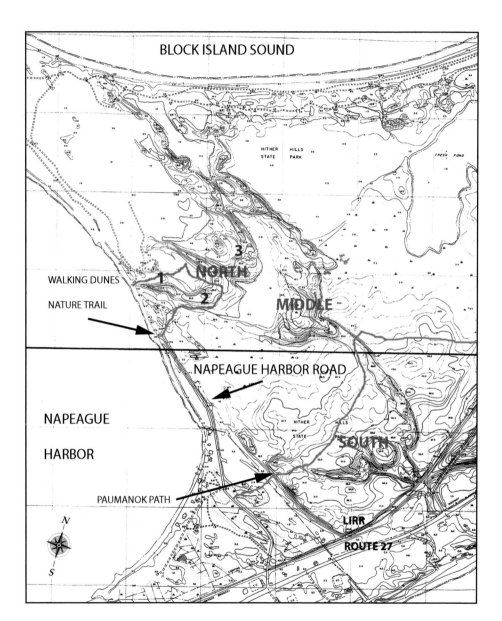

1972 Topographic Map with trails (in green) and North, South and Middle Walking Dunes.

scale: 1" = 1,000 ft

These topographic measurements are somewhat misleading if one assumes that these numbers represent the actual thickness of dune sand. A close examination of the topographic map and the Soil Conservation Service's Suffolk County Soils map reveals that portions of the South and Middle Dunes sit atop elevated glacial deposits. A visit to this area by way of the Paumanok Path reveals large rocks and boulders, material called glacial erratics that could only have been placed here by the glacial ice sheet. These are found in the vicinity of the 50 ft contour. Therefore, the wind-driven sand deposits that form the South Dune have a maximum thickness of approximately 40 ft. This has been confirmed by GPR (ground-penetrating radar) surveys (Davis and Cangelosi, 2005).

This 40 ft maximum thickness figure closely matches the 42 ft maximum height of the North Dune, which is nearly surrounded on all sides by marsh and swamp areas registering a height of less than 3 feet above mean sea level (amsl). The Middle Dune's maximum height of 56 ft is located adjacent to and close by an area of glacial deposits that have an elevation of 15 ft amsl, making the maximum thickness of this dune also approximately 40 ft.

It appears that all three dunes have a uniform thickness. Yet, over time, each of the three Walking Dunes has developed very distinct characteristics based on a combination of factors including age, development of stabilizing vegetation, protection from the northwesterly wind, human impact, and underlying topography.

The South Dune, assumed to be the oldest, has extensive forest cover and has shown negligible movement over at least the past 160 years.

Although individual Pitch Pines can be found scattered throughout Montauk, the Walking Dune Pitch Pine forest marks the eastern extent of this forest type on Long Island.

Its outer flanks, as well as the area surrounding it, are forested with oaks and hickories. Its inner flanks, excluding the dune ridge top, are covered with Pitch Pine.

This sharp demarcation in forest type is related to soils. In order to germinate, Pitch Pine seeds need to be in full sun and in contact with stable, mineral soils (e.g., stationary sand with no organic humus or leaf litter). In the Walking Dunes, these conditions are limited to areas of the parabolic dunes that have stabilized and are not cast in shade by the adjacent forest.

Although the same conditions are also found along much of the ridge top of the South and Middle Dunes, Pitch Pines have not colonized

Unusual Oak shapes, formed by the wind and shifting sands, found on the ridge tops of the Middle and South Dunes.

Pollen-bearing sacs adorn Pitch Pine's lower limbs.

these areas. The narrow ridge tops of both the Middle and South Dunes are vegetated with stunted, unusually shaped oaks. This is puzzling, but a clue was found in the growth form of these oaks--they had clearly been sculpted by the wind.

Pitch Pine seeds are small, light, and have a wing-like structure that enhances their dispersal by the wind. The pine seeds, easily wind-blown, were swept clear of the ridge tops before they were able to sprout. The much heavier acorns, most likely transported to and buried on the ridge by squirrels, chipmunks and mice, stayed put and germinated. Wind and the droughty dune soils have worked these oak trees into interesting photogenic specimens.

Where the northwesterly winds have completely removed all the dune sands and re-exposed the pre-dune glacial soils, a maritime oak-holly forest became established. The exception to this is found where the glacial till is at or below the water table. There, freshwater wetland species dominate, including Tupelo and Red Maple trees.

The Middle Dune, like the South Dune, is largely forested. Although comparisons of aerial photographs over the 58 year period between 1938 and 1996 show a net movement of over 56 ft, most of that southwesterly advance occurred over the earlier part of those years. Today the Middle Dune is quite stable.

The area inside its U-shaped dune ridge is vegetated by Pitch Pine, except for the low-lying areas where the water table is at or near the surface. There, as is the case with the South Dune, a mix of freshwater wetland vegetation dominates: Tupelo and Red Maple trees, Winterberry Holly, Sweet Pepperbush and Swamp Azalea shrubs, Cranberry vines, ferns, and a variety of sedges and rushes.

Tupelo leaves, and fruit (below), which is rich in lipids, a high-energy food available to birds during the fall migration.

33

When not in a forest setting, Pitch Pine's lower branches will grow horizontally as far as the tree is tall, a growth form called "skirting."

A young Pitch Pine growing in the cranberry bog. Although most competitive in dry, sandy soils, Pitch Pines can tolerate periodic inundation as the water table fluctuates, but not year-round immersion in the water.

Leaves and the wind-pollinated flowers of an Oak in May.

Along the eastern side of the Middle Dune's outer flanks, typical maritime oak-holly hardwoods dominate, except where a 500 foot-long section of the dune forms a horn jutting into Fresh Pond's extensive shrub swamp. The dune's low southern flank is vegetated on both sides, inner and outer, with Pitch Pines.

The North Dune is the least vegetated and least stable of the three. This dune has moved over 660 ft in a southeasterly direction between 1938 and 1996, for an average rate of advance of 11.48 ft per year over that period. This yearly average rate, however, masks the fact that the rate of advance has changed dramatically over that time frame. Between 1930 and 1955, the rate was calculated at 26.2 ft per year; more recently, between 2001 and 2004, the rate of advance diminished to 5.7 ft per year (Davis and Cangelosi, 2005).

When wet, the sweet-scented flowers of Sweet Pepperbush can be worked into a lather and used as a soap substitute, giving rise to two other common names for this shrub: Poor Man's Soap and Soapbush.

A low-growing sedge (Cyperus spp.) dominates the wet sand bordering the cranberry bog.

Swamp Azelia in early summer

Swamp Azelia in autumn, with a lichen--Old Man's Beard--on branches (left of center).

Wind-blown sand from the North Dune is slowly filling in a freshwater marsh.

In the Wake of the Dunes

As the forty-foot tall dunes moved, they smothered and eventually killed all the vegetation lying in their path. First to succumb were the low herbaceous plants and shrubs. Some of the taller shrubs and trees have displayed a remarkable ability to survive partial burial. A Button-bush, a woody shrub normally found growing in shallow freshwater, thrives on the leading edge of the North Dune despite most of the plant, approximately seven of its ten feet, being buried. Only the upper six feet of a thirty foot-tall Grey Birch protrude from the same dune.

The root systems of these wetland plants are immersed in the water table beneath the dune, and their survival is enhanced by the porous and sterile dune soil that inhibits bacterial and fungal growth. In the future, when the moving ridge of the dune is likely to cover their highest limbs completely, these plants will also succumb, as was the case with the twenty-foot-tall Tupelo tree growing alongside the Grey Birch.

Although they were completely buried for at least ten years, the lower portions of these trees sometimes remain upright and intact to emerge in the dune's wake as the "Phantom Forest." An interpretive sign (see next page) describing the origin and significance of these standing dead trees was erected in an attempt to prevent the loss of these unique relics to bonfires. Unfortunately, few of them remain.

Oak partially buried by sand.

THE PHANTOM FOREST

THIS AREA ONCE CONTAINED A FOREST OF PITCH PINE AND OAK. AS THE WALKING DUNE MOVED THROUGH THE AREA, ALL THE TREES WERE COMPLETELY BURIED UNDER THE SAND, AND NOW ALL THAT REMAINS OF THE FOREST ARE THE DEAD TREES YOU SEE HERE. AS THE DUNE CONTINUES MOVING IN A SOUTHEASTERLY DIRECTION, MORE TREES WILL BE UNCOVERED. PLEASE DO NOT DISTURB THE INTERESTING REMNANTS OF THE OLD FOREST.

Remnant of the forest overrun by the dune

The Role of the Wind

Wind plays a major role in shaping both the overall species composition of a region's flora and the form of its individual plants. This is particularly evident in coastal areas where the "fetch," or distance the wind blows unobstructed by land, can stretch for many miles over the surrounding bays or ocean. Wind impacts vegetation by several means, the most obvious being the simple act of drying out plant material.

Plant leaves are solar collectors whose function is to capture sunlight and utilize that energy to manufacture complex carbohydrates from simple compounds: carbon dioxide and water. The carbon dioxide is drawn in from the air via tiny pores, called stomata, in the leaf surface. Most plants gather water from the soil and send it along to the leaves via a system of interconnected tubes called xylem. A by-product of this photosynthetic process, fortunately for us, is oxygen, which escapes the same way carbon dioxide entered: via the stomata.

Water vapor can also escape from the leaf by way of the stomata. That's not a problem for plants growing in a very wet climate or those whose roots have access to the water table or moist soil. But for plants inhabiting porous dune sands in a climate that experiences midsummer droughts, the loss of water vapor is problematic. Add wind, which greatly accelerates water loss through the stomata, and the impact is serious.

Wind also influences coastal vegetation by transporting salt spray inland from the surface of the ocean and bay. The term "salt spray" refers to the fine mist generated by breaking waves and carried shoreward by the sea breeze, dampening beach towels and clothing and leaving a thin film on sunglasses. The term also refers to an invisible vapor that is not easily detected, one that can be transported far inland by even a light wind, and that is perhaps more accurately described by the term "saltwater vapor."

Plants that do not grow in the lee side of a dune (the side sheltered from the wind) or in the lee of other plants, become coated with a film of saltwater when exposed to the salt-laden wind. Unless accompanied by rain, this film eventually evaporates, leaving behind tiny crystals of sodium and chloride ions that can penetrate and kill the leaves and buds of most plants. Since the film coating is usually limited to the upper and windward portions of the plant, the end result is selective pruning that gives many coastal shrubs and trees a distinctive low, sprawling shape not found elsewhere in their range.

A third wind-related plant stress occurs in conjunction with sand. Even a slow ten-miles-per-hour wind can move most of the sand grains that are found on the beaches and dunes. Windblown sand can bury plants and damage their leaves, similar to the action of a sandblasting machine. On a very windy day, it is not unusual for the blowing, stinging sand to be uncomfortable enough to drive people off the beach.

Microenvironments on the dune's flank: Sand erosion on the upper slopes prevents American Beachgrass colonization. The mid-slope area has enough sand deposition to support lush Beachgrass growth, while the dead stalks of Beachgrass and small clumps of Beach Heather on the lower slope (foreground) show that this area has stabilized.

Sand

Sand grains are minerals that have been broken down from rock, a process involving several different physical and chemical mechanisms over many years. In this area, beach sands are very light colored, reflecting the predominance of a glass-like mineral called quartz, which accounts for 90% of the sand. Quartz, a very hard and nearly indestructible material, is the principal mineral of the earth's crust, and the main component of granite. Granite is the most common rock in the New England mountains where glaciers scoured, scraped, and carried rock and sand south to form the terminal moraine we now call Long Island.

A close look at the sand on Long Island beaches reveals a number of other colors. The light tan mineral is feldspar, purple is garnet, mica sparkles like tiny pieces of a mirror, and the greenish-black grains are hornblende. A small magnet is useful to separate out the tiny black grains of magnetite that resemble the filings in the game "Etch-a-sketch."

Each of these minerals has its own density. A strong steady wind can remove the lighter minerals, such as quartz, leaving behind pretty purple and black patterns on the beach made by the heavier minerals magnetite and garnet.

Many visitors comment on the orange-colored sand found on the eastern shore of Napeague Harbor near the Walking Dunes. This is most striking when low tide exposes the band of sand lying in the intertidal zone. A close examination reveals that both sand and rocks in the intertidal zone are orange-colored, the result of staining by iron oxides precipitating out of the groundwater.

Photo by Elsa Blum

Napeague Harbor's rust-colored intertidal zone is caused by the flow of iron-rich groundwater from the Hither Woods aquifer into the harbor.

45

The large lens of fresh groundwater underlying the 3,000 acres of preserved forest collectively known as Hither Woods is as thick as 150 feet in places (from the top of the water table extending vertically down to the interface with salt water). Near its edges, where the lens thins dramatically, this freshwater seeps south into the Atlantic Ocean, west into Napeague Harbor, north into Napeague Bay and Block Island Sound, and east into Fort Pond. The freshwater lost horizontally via seepage is replaced by precipitation filtering vertically down through the leaf litter and soil. Unlike the fresh groundwater seeping into the ocean and large, open bodies of water such as Napeague Bay and Block Island Sound, the fresh groundwater reaching a semi-enclosed, shallow embayment like Napeague Harbor significantly lowers salinity levels. This process creates an environment well-suited for the growth

and development of many juvenile marine organisms, and also creates prime conditions for spawning among many others. Rivulets of freshwater can actually be seen at low tide in the intertidal zone of Napeague Harbor's eastern shore.

Many assumed that the large, protected groundwater resource found beneath Hither Woods would be adequate to meet the future needs of Montauk, whose fresh drinking water supplies further east were inadequate in the summer months and suffering from overpumping and saltwater intrusion. However, Suffolk County Water Authority's test-well results revealed iron levels there that not only exceeded drinking water standards, but were interpreted as being too high to filter out without incurring excessive costs.

As the iron-rich freshwater seeps out of the ground, it comes into contact with oxygen. A reaction is triggered that results in the iron precipitating out of the groundwater and settling on the sand and rock substrate as a thin, rust-colored film of material called ferric hydroxide. Along the ocean and most bay beaches, wave action or strong currents wash the film away before it has a chance to accumulate. In some of our ponds and slow-moving rivers, this form of iron crystallizes to form bog iron, a resource harvested and forged here as late as the 1800s and crafted into iron anchors, chain, and other implements.

Wind sorts the common minerals found in dune sand (the light-colored quartz, purple garnet and black magnetite) according to their different densities, creating striking patterns on the sand's surface.

Exposed to the full force of the north winds, the inner slopes of the North Dune experience too much wind erosion and are largely devoid of vegetation.

Part 2: Plants of the Walking Dunes: Dune Plants

American Beachgrass

One could argue that there is no plant better adapted to the challenging conditions found on our coastal beaches and dunes than American Beachgrass (*Ammophila breviligulata*). Botanists have named it appropriately, for "*ammophila*" literally means "sandloving." Beachgrass is not only the dominant plant on our coastal dunes, it is the key to their actual formation.

Beachgrass acts like snow fencing, intercepting windblown grains of sand as they are carried off the beach, and causing them to accumulate around and partially bury its stems. Sand burial stimulates adventitious buds located on the stem to sprout and grow into horizontal stems called rhizomes. Rhizomes grow laterally up to 6 to 10 ft in one growing season, a reproductive strategy that enables Beachgrass to quickly colonize and stabilize areas of bare sand. From points along these rhizomes, new stems and leaves rise above the sand and new roots descend into it. You can often see which plants are connected to one another by a rhizome, as the stems form a perfectly straight line.

Beachgrass "rides" the building dune, unlike the snow fence which eventually gets buried as sand continues to accrete. Its network of fibrous roots and rhizomes provides an internal frame that supports and strengthens the dune. Although we think of a linear coastal dune as an elongated mound of sand grains, it would be interesting to dissect one to determine the volume of sand versus Beachgrass roots, rhizomes, and stems.

Wind, sandy soils, and windblown sand are plant stressors, and Beachgrass has developed some successful adaptations for each of them. The combination of the first two (wind, sandy soils) results in water stress, and Beachgrass addresses that via leaf design. One side of its leaf blade is smooth, the other has vertical ridges. The stomata, tiny pores through which water vapor can be lost, are located between the ridges such that on a hot, dry day, the leaf folds lengthwise. These ridges are brought together like an accordion, partially sealing off the stomata. In addition, the aerodynamics of the leaf ensure that the ridged, stomata-riddled side faces downwind.

On the eastern seaboard, sand is largely comprised of quartz, an extremely hard and abrasive yet light material that becomes airborne in winds as moderate as 10 mph. Wind-blown sand can create small cuts in a leaf's outer surface, causing it to lose moisture, dry out, and eventually die. To protect it from sandblasting, Beachgrass leaves contain silicon, a substance that gives them a tough, coarse feel.

American Beach Grass growing on top of the North Dune. The forested Middle Dune is in the background.

Wind pushing the bent tips of American Beachgrass' leaves scribes circles in the sand, giving rise to its other common name: Compass Grass.

Unlike most plants, Beachgrass not only survives periodic burial, it actually requires some degree of annual burial to thrive. Should the sand source be removed or greatly diminished, the once lush, tall Beachgrass plants lose vigor and may eventually die. Research has identified several possible explanations for this phenomenom: two relate to characteristics of the newly deposited sand, and two relate to characteristics of Beachgrass roots.

Wind-blown sand driven from the beach, up onto the dune, and deposited among the stems of Beachgrass is free of pathogenic nematodes and rich in nutrients from salt spray. The reverse is true of older, stablized sand. As noted above, Beachgrass' new roots are located above the older root system, and only develop in the presence of sand accretion. As Beachgrass' roots age, they become less efficient in absorbing nutrients from the sand. No sand burial means no new roots, inefficient nutrient uptake, and the degeneration of the entire plant.

New, young roots have also been found to exude carbohydrates into the sand, providing a source of carbon for nitrogen-fixing bacteria and enhancing their growth. Where no new roots are forming, growth of these beneficial bacteria decreases, nitrogen-fixation is diminished, and the vigor of Beachgrass declines. In their place, colonizing areas of bare sand between the brown stems of dead and dying Beachgrass, less hardy plants such as Beach Heather and Bearberry gain a foothold and become established. These, in time, may further stabilize the dune sands and enable Bayberry, Beach Plum and Pitch Pine seedlings to grow, an example of a gradual process of change called ecological succession.

Despite its need for accreting sand, even Beachgrass has its limits, and that line is found in the lee of portions of the North Dune where sand burial exceeds one foot per year. On the other extreme, many of the windward slopes (those forming the interior of its parabola) of the North Dune are devoid of any vegetation. These windward slopes are losing sand, a situation that most plants, even the hardy *Ammophila*, can't tolerate.

American Beachgrass colonizing the dune slope. Sand deposition and burial is too great for any other plant to survive here.

Beach Heather

Like American Beachgrass, Beach Heather *(Hudsonia tomentosa)* not only tolerates some degree of sand burial but actually grows best on sites where some sand deposition occurs. It cannot withstand the degree of burial that American Beachgrass can, and often replaces Beachgrass where conditions are stabilized and sand deposition is greatly diminished. In those cases, look for the dead stalks of Beachgrass among the mats of Beach Heather.

Since Beach Heather cannot tolerate salt spray, it will not replace Beachgrass on the primary dune slope facing the water or the dune ridge top. It can only compete with Beachgrass in the lee of the dune, where it is a dominant member of what is called the dune-heath community. There, along with Reindeer Lichen, Bearberry, Bayberry, Beach Plum, Carolina Sandwort, and a grass called Little Bluestem, it forms low, sprawling clumps of vegetation.

Beach Heather is an important pioneer plant in the back dunes. Its yellow flowers mature into tiny seeds that are easily dispersed by the wind, later germinating on bare sand and eventually forming large mats that help stabilize the area.

Beach Heather's tiny, scale-like, evergreen leaves cling tightly to its stems that grow low and outward in the form of a round cushion. Both its leaf form and growth habit are adaptations that enable it to thrive in its dry, windy environment. Although Beach Heather is an evergreen, its normally bright-green leaves take on a dull, brownish-gray color throughout the winter and in marginal growing conditions. In June, Beach Heather's profuse yellow flowers carpet the back dune area with color. As with Beachgrass, over time it helps stabilize the shifting sand and, in doing so, brings about its own demise, often being overtopped and shaded out by Bearberry.

Bearberry colonizing the edge of a blowout by way of its horizontal stems.
The small yellow flowers are Beach Heather.

Although attractive, Bearberry's red berries are mealy and tasteless. Each contains four or five seeds which need to pass through the acidic stomach of an animal in order to break down the tough seedcoat and germinate.

Bearberry

Bearberry *(Arctostaphylos uva-ursi)* grows so low to the ground that it often resembles a dense, trailing vine rather than a woody shrub. Its prostrate growth form is an adaptation for its habitat specialty: dry, windy sites. This slow-growing, long-lived, hardy plant is most abundant in the arctic tundra and along alpine ridges, but its range extends south where extremely dry, windy environments, such as those found among coastal dunes, give it a competitive edge. Other water conservation features are its small, leathery leaves and the tiny, wool-like hairs growing along its young twigs.

In order to germinate, the protective seed coats must be softened, or scarified, with acid, a process that takes place in the digestive systems of birds and mammals who feed on the large, red fruit. Although they look plump and attractive, and apparently have some value as a survival food, the fruits are tasteless. The fact that they persist through the winter is an indication that they are not a preferred food for most wildlife either. A possible exception may be the large omnivore for whom the plant is named (both the Greek genus name and Latin species name roughly translate to 'bear'). This creature with the non-discriminating palate will eat most anything. It was extirpated from Long Island many years ago. This plant is also known among Native Americans as Kinnikinnick, an Algonquian word for mixture. It refers to the use of its dried leaves, along with other ingredients that might include tobacco, as a mix for smoking. It's been reported that it alone is a poor substitute for tobacco.

Where protected from salt spray and sand burial, Bearberry spreads via rooting stems, called stolons, to form extensive mats over the dune sands. Vegetative reproduction from adjacent areas seems to be the most common means of colonizing disturbed areas in Napeague. Even among the sand roads now closed to vehicles, it is difficult to find evidence of new Bearberry plants having spread from seeds.

Scotch Broom, a member of the Pea family.

Beach Pea

Cranberry in bloom

Freshwater Wetland Plants

Cranberry and Sphagnum Moss

The low, ground-hugging, vine-like Cranberry plant growing in the wet soils and shallow freshwater wetlands of the Walking Dunes is the same species, *Vaccinium macrocarpon*, as the commercial Cranberry cultivated in large, managed wetlands on Cape Cod. Its delicate white flowers bloom in June and, if pollinated, mature to form a ripe berry in late October and early November. Since the cranberry plant is an evergreen, its tiny, oval leaves are visible throughout the year.

As the sun-loving Cranberry plants multiply, spread and thicken, they provide shade under which Sphagnum Moss (*Sphagnum palustre*) can grow. Sphagnum tends to hold water in its tissues, causing the bog to become more consistently moist, rather than fluctuating from wet to dry with rainfall. Constant moisture slows bacterial decomposition in the soil and causes peat to build up on the surface of the sand. Peat, in turn, holds more water than pure sand, and the bog becomes "squishy" underfoot.

Cranberry in bloom

Two Cranberries

61

Sphagnum Moss in winter

Insectivorous Plants

Ask anyone if they've ever heard of a plant that captures and eats insects and there's a good likelihood that they will reply, "Sure, the Venus Fly Trap!" In his book published in 1875, *Insectivorous Plants*, Charles Darwin wrote that the Venus Fly Trap was "the most wonderful plant in the world." Portrayed for many years in comics, movies, and cartoons, and readily available for purchase as a houseplant, the Venus Fly Trap (*Dionaea muscipula*) is the most recognizable and popular of the insectivorous plants.

Despite its popularity, few know its native origin. Most assume that such a bizarre and unusual plant must be from a far-away, exotic locale, perhaps the Amazon or Borneo. Actually, it is native to North and South Carolina and, until the second half of the 1700s, it was thought to be the only insect-eating plant in the world.

The Walking Dunes area is home to three species of insectivorous plants called Sundews (*Drosera* spp.). Unlike the very limited range of the Venus Fly Trap, Sundews grow on all continents except Antarctica. And unlike its more popular relative, the Sundews are quite small and easily overlooked in the field. A careful search will reveal them growing along the wet, sandy edges of the cranberry bog.

The three species are distinguished by leaf shape. The Thread-leaved Sundew (*D. filiformis*) is the easiest to find in the field, as it has long, narrow leaves that reach four to twelve inches above the bog. The tiny round (wider than long) and spoon shaped (longer than wide) leaves of Round-leaved Sundew (*D. rotundifolia*) and Spatulate-leaved Sundew (*D. intermedia*) respectively, form a basal rosette very close to the ground.

Spatulate-leaved Sundew

At first glance the leaves appear red-colored, but a close examination reveals that the leaf surfaces are green, reflecting the presence of chlorophyll pigment that enables the manufacture of carbohydrates via photosynthesis. The red appearance is due to the hair-like tentacles that cover the leaf surface. These tentacles are tipped with glands that secrete a clear, sticky substance resembling drops of dew. This both attracts insects, who mistake it for nectar, and traps them.

Once the insect lands on the leaf and becomes stuck in the glue-like dew, its sruggling movements are sensed by the plant and trigger differential growth among the tentacles in that area. The tentacles fold over the insect, further entrapping it as well as bringing it in closer contact with other tentacles. This growth among the tentacles is remarkably rapid: an outward pointing tentacle can turn 180° inward in less than one minute.

In some cases among the Round-leaved and Spatulate-leaved Sundews, the leaf itself may fold to help trap the insect. Movement by the struggling insect is critical in triggering tentacle growth and leaf folding. This ensures that energy is not wasted by debris (sand, pollen, etc) landing on the tentacles, as rapid tentacle growth is limited to three times per growing season.

Thread-leaved Sundew in bloom

Once the insect is secured, digestive fluids, also secreted by the tentacle-like glands, begin digesting all but the insect's hard exoskeleton. The digested material is then absorbed through the glands and used to supplement nutrients absorbed from the soil by way of the root system. Sundews do not require insect meals to survive. But research has shown that in bogs with very limited soil nutrients, Sundews that capture insects have more vigorous growth.

Despite his fascination with the Venus Flytrap, many of Darwin's experiments with insectivorous plants were carried out on Sundews. Toward the end of his 15 year-long studies with this plant, Darwin's wife was quoted, "I suppose he hopes to end in proving it an animal."

Thread-leaved Sundew

Trapped Moth

Thread-leaved Sundews. The leaves' sticky substance resembles drops of dew which attracts and traps insects.

Orchids

Within the plant kingdom, no group of plants can match the orchids in popularity and interest, which sometimes reaches almost mystical levels. Throughout human history, orchids have been prized, painted, photographed and, to the detriment of local populations, collected. Botanist Ann Johnson recorded five orchid species in the Walking Dunes area: three in freshwater wetland habitat and two in the understory of the Pitch Pine forest.

The anatomy of the orchid's intricate flower is the product of a long evolutionary history that coincides with the body size, weight, and shape of specific insect pollinators. The most common and best-known of our local orchids is the Pink Lady's Slipper or Moccasin Flower *(Cypripedium acaule)*. Its unusual flower has an entrance, two exits, and pollen-bearing and pollen-receiving structures, all specifically designed to promote pollination by medium-sized Bumblebees.

The Pink Lady's Slipper's flower petals are fused to form a sac. Bees are attracted to the flower's pink color and scent, but they are really interested in collecting the nectar they suspect is inside. A bee enters the sac by way of a slit-like funnel opening. This opening folds inward and narrows such that, once inside, the bee can't exit that way. Instead, a pathway of hairs (providing a good foothold on the slippery interior), colored lines and light from two small exit holes directs the bee to the back and top of the flower.

The bee, having been fooled and not finding any significant nectar source on which to feed, climbs to one of the exit holes and comes in contact with a sticky pad. This is the stigma, which receives any pollen the bee might be carrying on its back, and in doing so pollinates the plant.

Photo by Mike Bottini

Pink Lady's Slipper

Just outside each exit hole is a pollen-bearing structure, or anther. Anthers are positioned to coat the hairs on the bees' backs as they move into position to take flight, after which they transport the pollen to another Lady's Slipper.

This beautiful orchid is found in the Walking Dunes' oak and pine forests, and also grows in some backyards on eastern Long Island where homeowners have left the native vegetation intact. A perennial, the Lady's Slipper can live up to one hundred years, but does not flower every year. During that maximum one hundred year lifespan, it will bloom at most twenty times and only produce seed in five of those years.

Other unique examples of flower design matching a particular insect pollinator's size are the Grass Pink *(Calopogon tuberosus)* and Rose Pogonia *(Pogonia ophioglossoides)*, two similar-looking orchids found in the peatlands and freshwater marshes of the Walking Dunes. As with the Lady's Slipper, medium-sized bees, in this case Carpenter Bees, Solitary Bees, and Bumblebees, are the correct size and weight to perform the intricate act of pollination.

The bees are initially attracted to the pink flowers. Both orchids have hair-like filaments on one of their flower petals: the upper petal on the Grass Pink and the lower petal on the Rose Pogonia. The hair-like filaments absorb ultraviolet light and resemble stamens, both features that entice bees to land in search of nectar. Rose Pogonia does provide a small amount of nectar, but Grass Pink does not.

Grass Pink

Grass Pink's modified flower petal is hinged, and the bee's weight causes the petal to bend down until its back presses against the anther and stigma below. If the bee is carrying a pollen package, it will come in contact with the stigma and pollinate the plant; if not, its back will press against the anther and receive a sticky pollen sac.

Pink Lady's Slipper's and Grass Pink's pollination strategies rely on deception, since none of these plants reward the pollinator with food in the form of nectar. The bees eventually learn that the very attractive flowers do not contain nectar, and among a colony of these orchids the deception only works as long as there is a fresh supply of new, unsuspecting recruits. Despite its intricate floral adaptations designed to attract specific pollinators, studies have shown that fewer than ten percent of all Pink Lady's Slipper flowers get pollinated in most years.

Grasspink, Rose Pogonia, and Dewberry

Pollinated orchids form a fruit pod by the end of the summer. The pod dries out and splits to release as many as ten thousand tiny, dust-like seeds that are dispersed by the wind. The bulk of most plants' seed is composed of stored food (called endosperm) for the germinating plant. Most orchid seeds are tiny and easily carried by the wind because they lack endosperm.

To compensate, the tiny orchid seed must come in contact with a particular species of fungus. The fungus provides nutrients that enable the seed to germinate, and over the first two or three years that it takes for its leaves to develop significant size, the young plant appears to have a parasitic relationship with the fungus.

Rose Pogonia

Phragmites

Phragmites' tough stems persist as dead stalks through the winter.

An easily recognizable plant with hollow, bamboo-like stems that can reach over ten feet in height and are crowned with an attractive plume-like inflorescence, Phragmites *(Phragmites australis)* is one of the most widespread grasses in the world and found on every continent except Antarctica. It is also found in nearly every water body on eastern Long Island. This was not always the case. Naturalist Roy Latham first reported Phragmites growing in Orient, Long Island, in 1900 and on the South Fork in 1920.

Recent research shows that Phragmites grew in the Northeast as many as three thousand years ago, but it was not as ubiquitous as it is today. Botanical inventories from the 1800s and early 1900s do not mention Phragmites at sites on Long Island that today have extensive stands of the grass. The appearance and dominance of Phragmites at many of our local marshes seems to date back to the early 1900s.

Phragmites' feathery plumes of tiny flowers are pollinated by the wind and develop into seeds.

Botanists have confirmed that this relatively recent surge in growth is attributed to a non-native genotype of Phragmites introduced to the metropolitan New York area from outside the U.S. Several physical characteristics have now been identified that distinguish it, at least among botanists with a practiced eye, from our native race. But more importantly, several distinguishing growth characteristics have been identified for the exotic race-- it is tolerant of a wider range of soil types, and it is much more aggressive, with growth via horizontal stems (rhizomes) measured in meters, not inches, per year.

The late afternoon light accentuates Phragmites' seed heads in the fall.

Writing about the issue in 1957, Roy Latham's words still ring true today: "The Phragmites is a beautiful grass greatly admired by people who enjoy the landscape. Most naturalists have a dislike for it."

Some detest it as an intruder. The botanist finds little worth searching for within its limits. The collecting entomologist finds it unproductive, difficult to get through to work in. The birdman fares somewhat better, for the thick stands of this reed form shelters for winter sparrows, wrens and rails.

Phragmites is a valuable plant in terms of stabilizing shorelines and preventing sediment and pollutants from entering adjacent water bodies. Natural resource managers, however, are concerned that its spread results in an overall decrease in plant diversity, as well as diversity of fauna dependent on those replaced plants for food and shelter.

Much research has focused on methods to eradicate, or at least slow the growth of Phragmites, and some techniques (controlling water levels, excavating the plants and their deep root systems, applying herbicides) have been implemented here. More Phragmites control projects are sure to be implemented in the future but, like it or not, this hardy plant will continue to be a dominant part of the East End landscape for many years to come.

Highbush Blueberry

Highbush Blueberry's red-tinted buds and new growth.

Highbush Blueberry's fruit

More Plants in the Walking Dunes Area

Bayberry

Most everyone interested in nature, and keen on learning more about it, eventually realizes the necessity of using the awkward but precise scientific labels for species of plants and animals. For example, there are at least four native grasses, and one woody plant (the low shrubs growing profusely in the dunes called *Hudsonia tomentosa* that go by the common name "poverty grass."

Northern Bayberry, a common shrub found in many habitats, is unusual in that it is listed under two different scientific names, *Myrica pensylvanica* and *Morella pensylvanica*. It is easily identified at any time of the year by its aromatic (when crushed) leaves and twigs. Although the leaves can be used to flavor soups and stews, the plant that produces the bay leaves found in most kitchen spice racks is from the Mediterranean, with Turkey being one of the main suppliers. Commercial use of our native Bayberry is limited to its gray-blue berries that, when boiled, yield a wax which makes a pleasantly fragrant candle.

The wax coating on its small hard berry makes it difficult to digest. But those that can, such as the Tree Swallow and the Yellow-rumped Warbler, are rewarded for their efforts since the wax has a high lipid, or fat, content. The berries of the *Myrica* (or *Morella)* genus are such an excellent source of high-quality energy for the Yellow-rumped Warbler that, where these plants are abundant, the birds can overwinter and survive further north than any other warbler species in North America.

Bayberry in winter

Bayberry has some other interesting characteristics worth noting. Its roots, in association with bacteria, develop nodules that enable the conversion of nitrogen from the air into compounds that its roots can absorb and utilize in the manufacture of proteins. It is not clear whether the nitrogen-fixing ability of Bayberry benefits other plants growing nearby, and some researchers have speculated that Bayberry excretes chemicals into the soil that inhibit the growth of other plants, a strategy to reduce competition for nutrients and water called allelopathy.

Plant flowers are classified as either perfect (each flower structure contains both male and female parts) or imperfect (there are separate male and female flowers). The latter group is further subdivided into those species that have both male and female flowers on each plant (called monoecious species) and those that have only one type of flower, male or female, on each plant (called dioecious species). An example of the latter, mentioned elsewhere in this book, is the hollies.

Bayberry's flowers are imperfect, but the plants can be either dioecious or monoecious. Obviously, only those with female flower structures can become pollinated and develop fruit, so you may encounter Bayberry plants that never produce berries. I have noticed that the plants growing in the shade of the forest, in addition to having a more "leggy" form than those inhabiting sunny sites, do not produce berries. It is unlikely that all these forest-dwelling plants only have male flowers; I suspect that the shaded environment does not provide enough energy for plants to reproduce via flowering.

Bayberry's pollen-bearing male flowers

Beach Plum's long stamens are tipped with tiny yellow anthers that contain pollen.
If pollinated, the flowers will mature into delicious plums that make an ecellent jam.

Black Cherry and Beach Plum

Two members of the cherry (*Prunus*) genus commonly found in the Walking Dunes are Black Cherry *(Prunus serotina)* and Beach Plum *(Prunus maritima)*. Both have horizontal lines, called lenticels, marking their bark and most can be identified at a distance by the presence of abnormal, black swellings, called black knots, on their twigs and branches. The black knots are galls that formed as a result of infection by the fungus *Dibotryon morbosum*, which causes localized, rapid division of plant cells and disfigurement, over a period of two years. If the gall completely encircles the branch, that portion above the gall can be killed. Some references claim the fungus can eventually kill the entire plant, but I have not seen evidence of this in the Walking Dunes.

Both plants are hosts for another organism that gives the plants a distinctive appearance: the Eastern Tent Caterpillar (*Malacosoma americanum*). By late spring, many Beach Plums and Black Cherries here are adorned with the caterpillar's characteristic silken webs.

The conspicuous Black Knot fungal growth is so common on Black Cherries that it is a useful identification feature for that species.

The pinkish/red growths on the surface of these Beach Plum leaves are galls.

Beach Plum never grows larger than a small shrub. On good soils, Black Cherry can reach heights of over 60 feet and, because of its very attractive wood, is an important lumber tree. But in the sandy soils of the Walking Dunes its growth is generally limited to that of a large shrub.

Despite their similarities, a practiced eye can identify each in the field. Black cherry has shiny, oblong, finely-toothed leaves, while Beach Plum's are smaller, more oval, and duller. By mid-summer, a close look at the underside of a Black Cherry leaf will reveal orange "fuzz"

Beach Plum in early June

growing along the midrib, a feature that is lacking among the Beach Plums. Note that Black Cherry has a longer leaf stalk, or petiole, that causes the leaves to appear, from a distance, to droop on their twigs. Both have similar white flowers that blossom in May and June. Black Cherry's flowers form in clusters along a drooping stem at the tips of its branches, a configuration called a terminal raceme. If pollinated, these mature into pea-sized, blue-black fruits. Beach Plum's flowers form individually, back from the tip of its branches, and mature into grape-sized, purplish fruits that make an excellent jam. Both fruits are relished by a wide variety of birds and mammals, "so much so," according to William Harlow's book *Trees of the Eastern and Central United States and Canada*, "that it was practically impossible to collect a complete cluster [of the Black Cherry fruits] for photographing."

Black Cherry after its white-petaled blossoms have fallen and before the pollinated ovaries have matured into fruit.

Black Cherry's fruit will turn a deep purple when ripe.

Virginia Creeper and Dewberry

Found at the start of the nature trail are two plants that are often confused with Poison Ivy. Both Virginia Creeper (*Parthenocissus quinquefolia)* and Dewberry *(Rubus* spp.) are vines with compound leaves, but there the similarity ends. One of Dewberry's most distinguishing features is its stem, which is adorned with bristles or thorns. Be sure to check for these on the older parts of its trailing stem, as the new growth among some species is smooth.

Another distinguishing feature of Dewberry is its flower. Unlike the inconspicuous blossoms of Poison Ivy and Virginia Creeper, Dewberry has five-petaled white flowers up to an inch in width that resemble those of the Wild Strawberry. Its blackberry-like fruit is small but tasty.

Virginia Creeper leaves in late spring

Dewberry

Both Dewberry and Virginia Creeper have leaflets with uniformly serrated edges. The latter, also called Woodbine, is easily separated from Dewberry and Poison Ivy because it has five leaflets. Virginia Creeper produces small clusters of berries presented on reddish stems. This fruit, black when ripe, has a high lipid (fat) content and is much sought after by fall migrants needing an energy-rich meal. Unlike the berries of Poison Ivy and the Hollies (*Ilex* spp.) that are passed over until late fall and winter because of their low lipid content, the berries of the Virginia Creeper are usually gone by the end of the fall migration.

The foliage of this commercially available plant turns crimson red as early as late August, joining the Pepperidge and Poison Ivy as one of the earliest and most handsome native plants to announce the turn of the seasons.

Dewberry

The Hollies

Three species of Holly, two shrubs and one tree, are found in the Walking Dunes. Most familiar among them is the American Holly (*Ilex opaca*) whose prickly, broad evergreen leaves and bright red berries are a welcome splash of color in the winter landscape, as well as a symbol of the Christmas holiday.

Among the broad-leaved evergreen trees, American Holly is the hardiest and found furthest north. Most broad-leaved evergreen trees are found in the south and the tropics. Where the winter season brings snow, subfreezing temperatures, and frozen ground, evergreen leaves need to be designed to shed snow and minimize water loss (water vapor escapes through pores in the leaf called stomata). For these reasons, evergreen trees in snow country have evolved needle-shaped leaves. Eastern Long Island is near the northern limit of American Holly's range, which extends another hundred miles north into coastal Massachusetts.

While hardy, it is also extremely slow growing, a characteristic found throughout its range but more pronounced here in its northern reaches. Its slow growth is reflected in growth rings that are often so close together as to be nearly indiscernible.

Inkberry Holly

American Hollies are scattered throughout Hither Woods, but unusually large numbers of them are found in the forested area north of Fresh Pond and east of the Walking Dunes. The reason for this unequal distribution may be related to this species' susceptibility to fire. Even a light ground fire can fatally damage its thin bark, and there has been no shortage of conflagrations, large and small, since the LIRR (Long Island Railroad) was extended east through Hither Woods to Montauk in 1895. Most of these forest fires are thought to have originated as sparks from passing trains, particularly over the years that the locomotives were steam-powered. Separating the existing large stands of American Holly from the LIRR, and protecting them from fire damage, are Fresh Pond and the extensive swamp to its south and west.

A shade-tolerant tree, American Holly fares well in the understory of oaks and hickories on eastern Long Island, rarely climbing high enough to join them in the forest canopy. An exception to this is found at the Sunken Forest on Fire Island, where American Holly forms an unusual maritime climax forest with another understory tree, Shadbush (*Amelanchier canadensis*), and one generally listed as a pioneer or early successional species, Sassafras (*Sassafras albidum*). There, cores have revealed that some of the hollies are two hundred years old.

Thanks in part to the thick waxy coating on its leaves, American Holly is surprisingly tolerant of salt spray and, in the rare instances where moist or clay-rich soils are found near the ocean (as is the case along the Paumanok Path at Turtle Cove), diminutive, wind-pruned hollies thrive. It would be interesting to age these tenacious specimens that resemble the severely wind-sculpted Black Spruces and Balsam Firs comprising the krummholz zone of alpine summits in New England.

A sapling American Holly growing beneath a canopy of oaks.

The inconspicuous white flowers of Winterberry Holly develop into conspicuous bright-red fruits that persist into the winter months.

Prickly Pear Cactus

Prickly Pear (*Opuntia humifusa*) is our only native cactus. Although there are not many of these unusual plants in the Walking Dunes area, one of the easiest places to locate a Prickly Pear Cactus is along the Paumanok Path just east of where it crosses Napeague Harbor Road.

As in other members of this group of desert specialists, the Prickly Pear Cactus has a large water storage capacity and a very low surface area-to-volume ratio to reduce water loss. The large, chlorophyll-filled pads where photosynthesis occurs are not leaves but modified stems and branches. The leaf structure has evolved into thin spines, which grow from small, wart-like nodes scattered over the pads. Just above the spines are very fine and tiny barbed spines that are unique to the *Opuntia* genus. These spines are more difficult to see, and much more difficult to remove once lodged in the skin. Its flower is anything but tiny. The two-to-three inch-wide yellow flowers bloom in early June, and mature to form a red and tasty fruit.

The pads of the Prickly Pear Cactus tend to orient their flat surfaces to the east or west, avoiding the more intense southern exposure. The Cactus grows low to the ground, a strategy that serves it well on our windy shores. These special adaptations come at a cost: Prickly Pear grows very slowly.

Salt Marsh Grass

A small band of salt marsh cordgrass survives on Napeague Harbor's east shoreline. A larger area of salt marsh thrives in the harbor's more sheltered southwest corner.

Coarse Reindeer Lichen growing among Bearberry, whose leaves have turned purple.

Lichens

Lichens are amazing organisms. They are found on all continents in the tropics and deserts, at both poles, on mountain peaks and in the intertidal zone. They can survive temperatures as high as 194°F and as low as –320°F. Lichens are the dominant vegetation in the coldest parts of the Arctic and Antarctic, on the highest mountain peaks, and in some of the hottest deserts. Nicknamed "nature's pioneers," lichens can colonize bare rock and are often the first plant-like forms to become established on newly exposed surfaces.

Biologists use the term "plant-like" to describe lichens because this unusual organism does not fit neatly into any existing classification system. Lichens are actually two distinct organisms, a fungus and an alga, growing in such close association that they form a separate organism. In doing so, the cells of each are so radically altered that, with the exception of blue-green algal cells, they no longer resemble the cells of the fungal and algal species from which they originated. In fact, the green algal cells of lichens are so altered that, in order to identify their species, they must be separated from the lichen in a lab and grown alone in a culture.

Biologists also use the term "symbiosis" to describe the fungal-algal relationship. The alga photosynthesizes and produces carbohydrates, supplying the fungus with food. The fungus' tiny threads, called hyphae, surround and protect each algal cell, enabling the algae to survive in environments where, were they in a free-living state outside of the lichen, they would perish. Lichens are often cited as a perfect example of mutualism, a symbiotic relationship in which both partners benefit with no adverse effect on one another. Irwin Brodo, one of the world's leading authorities on lichens and author of a book on

Long Island's lichens, writes that the relationship between the fungus and alga is complex, and in most cases the algae are actually parasitized and killed by the fungal cells. Fortunately, the algal cells can reproduce faster than the fungi can destroy them, but this arrangement hardly qualifies as mutualistic.

Fine Reindeer Lichen prefers to grow on the organic material of the forest floor, especially on carpets of pine needles.

Brodo found over 130 species of lichens on Long Island. Although they are easily overlooked, they are everywhere in the Walking Dunes. The cushion-like mats of several species of Reindeer Lichen (*Cladonia* spp. and *Cladina* spp., also known as Reindeer Moss) are a dominant feature of our dune landscape, colonizing many areas of bare sand. These comprise 90 percent of the winter diet of Caribou and Reindeer in the far north, but do not appear to be grazed by the member of the deer family found in the Walking Dunes — the Whitetailed Deer.

Usnea, or *Old Man's Beard*

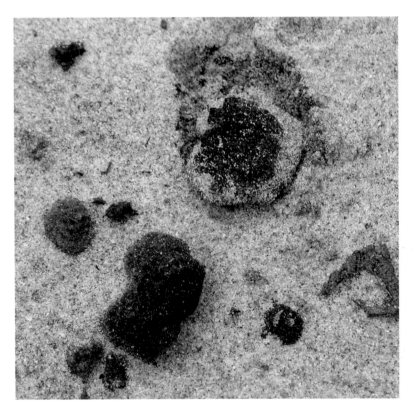

Tar Spot Lichen

Another common lichen found in the Walking Dunes is Tar Spot Lichen, listed under three different genus names: *Lecidea uliginosa, Placynthiella uliginosa,* and *Saccomorpha uliginosa.* As the name suggests, this unusual lichen resembles clumps of asphalt. In this case, the fungus' hyphae grow in among the sand grains and bind them together, incorporating the sand into the structure of the lichen. This is an excellent example of how lichens not only colonize the bare mineral sand, but stabilize and enrich it with organic material. It is difficult to find a single mature tree here that does not sport a growth of lichen on its bark. Many of these crustose forms of lichens are quite subtle and easily mistaken for the bark itself. Others resemble tufts of hair; these gray-green growths are appropriately named Old Man's Beard (*Usnea* spp.).

Lichens not only lack roots, they lack any root-like structure that allows them to absorb minerals, nutrients and water from the substrate on which they grow. Since they gain nothing from the material on which they sit, lichens are not limited by substrate and soil type as are most plants, a characteristic which enables them to grow on most anything. There is even a species of lichen found growing on the shells of Galapagos tortoises!

The lack of a root-like structure has a downside: all the lichen's nutrients and water for photosynthesis and growth come from the air. Lichens absorb moisture from rain, fog, and humidity. Nutrients are obtained from whatever happens to be dissolved in that moisture or lands on the lichen as ambient dust. This makes for extremely slow growth rates, which measure less than 0.15 inches per year for the crustose lichens found on tree bark, and between 0.06 – 0.4 inches per year for the Reindeer Lichens.

Lichens also lack water storage structures, tissues designed to move water around within the organism, and a waxy cuticle to slow water loss during a drought. This raises the question: how do they survive the often hot, dry and windy conditions found in the Walking Dunes? They simply go dormant. Lichens stored dry for twelve months resumed photosynthesis soon after being rewetted with no permanent damage to their algal cells!

This ability accounts for the simplest of several means of lichen reproduction and dispersal — small, dried fragments are broken off and dispersed by the wind. Other reproductive strategies are a little complicated. Several other forms of vegetative reproduction involve the formation of specialized structures that contain tiny bits of fungal hyphae wrapped around algal cells. When mature, these dust-like particles break off and are dispersed by wind, water, and wildlife.

Sexual reproduction, in which two individual lichens each contribute cellular material (a gamete) that fuses to form a zygote and a new individual lichen, does not occur. The only form of sexual reproduction takes place between the fungal components of two lichens. When their respective hyphae meet and fuse, fungal spores develop and are released. Only if these spores meet a suitable algal cell will a lichen form.

Although they lack roots, many lichens have specialized structures that anchor them in place. Many of the crustose lichens grow so closely in and among the tiny particles of their substrates, that they cannot be removed without also removing some of the substrate itself. Included is one species whose holdfast-like hyphae can penetrate several millimeters into granite. Many species that grow on rock also secrete chemicals that dissolve rock into its mineral components, and in doing so they help speed the natural process of weathering and soil formation.

Lichens produce over 600 secondary chemicals that are not directly related to their growth and metabolism. These chemicals serve as sunscreens (for the light-sensitive alga), anti-browsing agents (effective against small invertebrate browsers), and they inhibit seed germination and the growth of soil fungi and bacteria. Some have commercial use, such as the dye called litmus that changes color when exposed to solutions of varying pH. Most are acids, and although most are produced by the fungal component, the ability to manufacture these chemicals is greatly diminished when the fungi are isolated from the algal cells.

Old Oak trunk covered with Lichen.
Home of the Garter Snake shown on page 117.

Earth Star and Other Mushrooms

A surprising number and variety of mushrooms appear in the late summer and fall, even on the dune sands that seem completely devoid of any organic material on which fungi grow. Mushrooms are fungi's spore-bearing, reproductive structures, as well as their most evident and familiar parts. The bulk of the fungi is composed of tiny, thread-like bundles of hyphae called mycelia that are underground and hidden from view. Despite being inconspicuous and tiny, fungi mycelia play a very important role in the ecosystem. They secrete enzymes that digest complex organic material into simpler compounds that can then be absorbed. Those that derive nutrients from dead organic material are called saprophytes; those that digest living tissue are parasitic. The process of breaking down organic material is called decomposition. Through decomposition the surrounding plants are provided with a source of key nutrients which they can also absorb and utilize in growth and photosynthesis. In this way, fungi function as decomposers and recyclers.

One of the most conspicuous members of the fungi kingdom in the Walking Dunes is the Earth Star (*Geaster hygrometricus*). It belongs to a group of mushrooms, appropriately named puffballs, that have a closed cavity where the spores develop and ripen. As with other fungi, the mushroom forms when hyphae from two different fungi meet and fuse. When mature, the outer two layers of the mushroom split into four to twelve rays and the thin, pliable inner puffball develops a hole at its top. When it rains, the outer layers uncurl and open, exposing the puffball to rain drops that strike the surface and cause spores to "puff" out the opening. The tips of the unfurled rays sometimes bend back 180° to reach the ground and lift the Earth Star with enough force to sever it from the underground mycelium. During the next dry spell, the rays recurl around the now unattached puffball to form a round-shaped structure that is easily blown over the sand by wind. Spores are probably released along the way, but it appears that most of the one billion spores are released during wet weather. Due to their tough outer skin that does not easily degrade, Earth Stars, unlike other mushrooms, can be found throughout the year.

Earth Stars

Shelf Fungi

The familiar reproductive structures of fungi, the mushrooms, pop out of the sand while the underground mycelia, which play a key role as recyclers of nutrients in the ecosystem, remain hidden throughout the year.

Wildflowers

In addition to the blooming shrubs and wildflowers described earlier (black cherry, beach plum, beach pea, sundew, orchids), many other wildflowers grow in the Walking Dunes area.

Rose Rugosa flowers (above), and Vitamin C packed fruits called rose hips (below)

Sweet Everlasting

Sickle-leaved Goldenaster

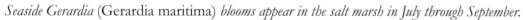

Seaside Gerardia (Gerardia maritima) *blooms appear in the salt marsh in July through September.*

Detached Gerardia flower

Goldenaster growing near Beach Heather

Part 3: Animals of the Walking Dunes Area

Fowler's Toad and Wolf Spider

A thermometer placed on the surface of sunlit, bare dune or beach sand can register as high as 150° F during the summer months. How do heat-sensitive animals cope with extreme temperatures? One solution is a behavioral adaptation: Avoid the high midday heat by being active only during the cooler temperatures of dawn, dusk and night. Another solution is to seek out cool, moist micro-environments in the duneland. The latter usually involves burrowing below the upper layer of hot, dry sand. Two curious examples of the dune faunal community that employ these strategies are the Fowler's Toad *(Bufo woodhousii fowleri)* and the Wolf Spider *(Geolycosa* spp.).

Outside of their long hibernation period (October through April), evidence of the Fowler's Toad's nocturnal wanderings among the sands of the Walking Dunes is everywhere in the form of its characteristic tracks. During the summer breeding season, its long (up to four seconds) mating call, best described as a nasal bleat "wha-a-a-a-a," can be heard from many of the shallow freshwater wetlands where it breeds. Peak breeding season is May and June. Depending on water temperature, the eggs can hatch in as little as two days and at most seven; the black tadpoles metamorphose into miniature four-legged adults over the course of another six weeks.

Fowler's Toad on Mike's hand

Toad tracks

103

Despite the relatively rapid rate of growth of eggs and larvae, many of the Fowler's Toads' breeding areas may completely dry out in some years before the tadpoles metamorphose. The ecological tradeoff is that these vernal pools cannot support fish predators.

This common but well-camouflaged and often overlooked creature is easily found in the summer months during the late afternoon and early evening hours when it hunts for insects. During the day it is generally inactive, having backed itself down into the cool layer of sand where it remains covered until dusk. Dozens of half-inch long, recently metamorphosed young-of-the-year may be encountered in August when they leave breeding pools and search for territories.

Another fascinating example, much easier to find once you know what to look for, is the Wolf Spider. These fierce-looking but harmless spiders can burrow as deep as three feet into the sand to escape the heat. The burrows are very distinctive, having perfect pencil-to-dime sized entrances with the sand grains held together by silk. Most people associate spiders with webs, but Wolf Spiders hunt their prey on the ground and on foot. In addition to having eight legs, Wolf Spiders have eight eyes. At night your flashlight might pick up the eerie, green eye-shine of its four largest eyes.

Photo from Wikipedia Commons

Wolf Spider showing six of its eight eyes.

Wolf Spider burrows

Tent Caterpillar

Conspicuous in the late spring and early summer landscape are the white silken masses of the Eastern Tent Caterpillar (*Malacosoma americanum*). Its tents are found on many species in the *Rosacea* family, particularly the cherries (*Prunus* spp.), apples (*Malus* spp.), and shadbush (*Amelanchier* spp.). In the Walking Dunes, tent caterpillars are most prevalent on the two common species of *Prunus*: Black Cherry (*Prunus serotina*) and Beach Plum (*Prunus maritima*).

The life cycle of this insect includes some interesting features and, since it is easily observed, makes an excellent subject of field study. From July through April, the eggs are visible as shiny, dark, inch-long masses, the texture of hard foam, that encircle small twigs. Surprisingly, the embryos begin development soon after the eggs are laid, and within three weeks (by August) the eggs contain fully-formed caterpillars.

The host plants of the Tent Caterpillar include Beach Plum and Black Cherry. This is a typical Tent Caterpillar nest.

The tiny caterpillars remain dormant in the eggs through the fall and winter. They have evolved to emerge when their host plant begins to leaf out, since the leaves are their only source of food during the larval stage. During this six-week period the larvae are essentially small feeding factories.

The air temperature at this time of year poses a challenge for the caterpillars, who require a minimum temperature of 59°F for digestion. Two adaptations for addressing this are body color and tent construction. The young larvae are black to best absorb heat from the sun, and by massing together in the sunlight on the tent surface they can significantly increase their body temperature. The communal tent is built of silk secreted from the larvae spinnerts and woven around a fork in the outer branches. The tent acts as a greenhouse, and for that reason it is oriented with its broadest side facing southeast and the early morning sun. Temperatures in the tent can be as much as 75°F higher than outside!

As they grow and the tent fills with frass (excrement) and molted skins, the caterpillars enlarge the structure by adding another layer of silk completely around the older tent so that, over time, it becomes a multi-layered unit. On a hot day, the caterpillars may seek the cooler, inner layers to avoid overheating. Another cooling behavior is to move to the shaded side of the tent, and dangle in the air hanging from the tips of their abdomens.

The tent has several other functions. It maintains a humidity level suitable for growth and molting, provides protection from predators, and serves as a staging area for feeding. The feeding function is facilitated by conspicuous silken paths that lead from the tent out along branches of the tree. Whenever a caterpillar leaves the tent to feed, it lays down a silk thread to find its way back. If its search for food leads to

105

a branch with lots of leaves, it lays down a pheromone on its return to the tent. This marker lets others in the tent know which route leads to a good foraging area. Careful observers may notice a bizarre thrashing motion among caterpillars massed on the tent's surface. Although the conspicuous movement would seem to draw attention to potential predators, the moving targets apparently ward off and intimidate some parasitic insects as well as the more timid predators Others, including many insectivorous birds that are busy feeding their young, avoid this abundant, easily captured source of calories. They are deterred by the caterpillar's toxicity, a result of its foraging on the cyanide-laden leaves of the Black Cherry.

Interestingly, no evidence has been found that the closely related Beach Plum or Shadbush produce hydrocyanic acid (although it has been documented in *Amelanchier alnifolia,* a western species of shadbush). One of the few birds that finds the Tent Caterpillar palatable is the cuckoo, both the Yellow-billed and Black-billed species. Neither is common in the Walking Dunes.

During its fifth instar, after its fourth molt, the caterpillars feed only under the cover of darkness. By early June, having completed their final molt and now fully grown, the caterpillars drop off their host trees and search for suitable sites (under a log, in a crevice) to spin their pupal sacs, or cocoons. They will spend two weeks there, emerging as early as late June as a reddish-brown or tan moth with an inch-long wingspan. The adult stage is very brief, at most a matter of days. Soon after she mates, the female lays a mass of 200-300 eggs on the branch of a suitable host tree, and dies.

While many Black Cherries and Beach Plums are completely stripped of leaves by these caterpillars, few actually perish. Trees and shrubs keep a supply of unopened leaf buds for emergencies. These adventitious buds will open soon after the caterpillars are finished feeding in early June, and enable the plant to survive another year.

Tent Caterpillar on Oak leaf

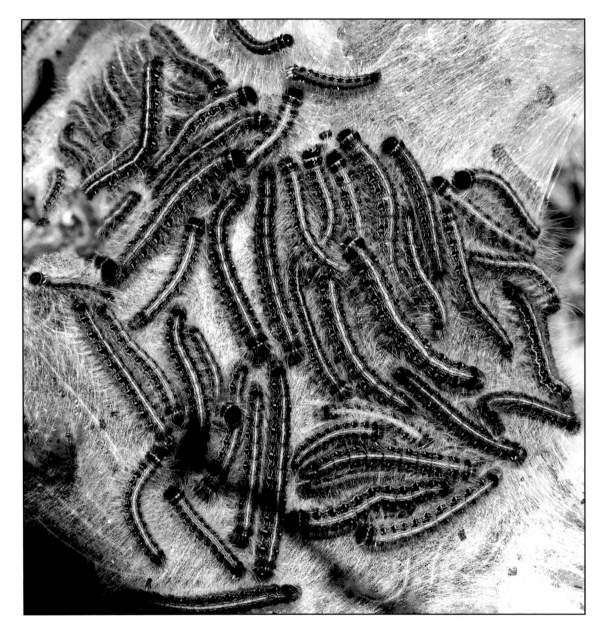

Tent Caterpillars basking on their silken tent

More Animals of the Walking Dunes Area

Lion's Mane Jellyfish

Fiddler Crab

Several pairs of Ospreys nest in the Napeague area. This female is returning to its nest with a small fish in the talons of its right foot.

Photo by Helen Pine

A Snowy Egret stalks the shallows of Napeague Harbor in search of small fish prey, while a Herring Gull looks on.

The long rear toe on the tracks indicates this is a perching bird, as opposed to the very short rear toes of ground-dwelling birds such as the Bobwhite Quail and many of our shorebirds.

Cottontail Rabbit droppings in the Beachgrass

The webbed feet of a gull or similar bird.

This turtle is crossing Napeague Harbor Road.

The Eastern Box Turtle resides in the forested areas of the Walking Dunes, but females often wander onto the sparsely vegetated sand in June while searching for suitable nesting sites.

Molted shells of Horseshoe Crabs

A Channeled Whelk covered with Slipper Shells

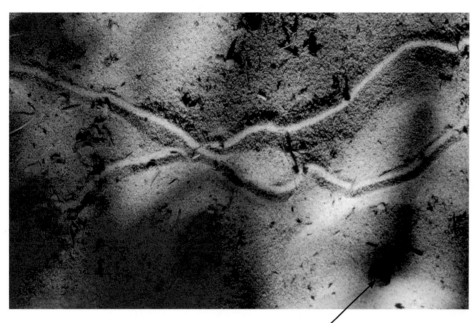

This commonly encountered track is actually made by an animal, the larva of the Antlion, as it moves mole-like just beneath the surface of the sand. Also known as a Doodlebug, its inverted conical 'pit trap,' in which it captures other insects, can be seen in the lower right.

pit trap

The Sand Locust is a common grasshopper in the Dunes. Its coloration so closely resembles sand that it is difficult to spot unless it moves.

The Piping Plover, an endangered species, nests on Goff Point and forages for food on the Napeague Harbor beach and intertidal zone.

A juvenile Great Black-backed Gull feasts on what's left of a fisherman's catch.

On the last day I photographed for this book, I saw a black and yellow snake — a harmless Garter Snake — sunning itself in front of an oak stump's large opening. As my shutter clicked, the snake looked up and soon disappeared inside its home. My first and only snake in the Dunes! I felt rewarded for my hard work over the many years of this project. See a large photo of the oak stump, covered with lichen, in the Lichens chapter, on page 96.

Minnows with their shadows at low tide.

Harmless Garter Snake

Author Biographies

Ruth Formanek, photographer and psychologist, has been a keen observer of nature and human behavior since childhood. A professional photographer, Ruth has had several solo exhibitions and often participates in group shows. A clinical psychologist, she is a retired Professor of Elementary Education at Hofstra University where she taught Child Development for over 30 years. During that time she was active in research projects and in the American Psychological Association, wrote papers and edited books on children's and women's cognitive and clinical issues. Ruth lived in Amagansett for 25 years where she discovered the Walking Dunes to be a photographer's dream. Currently a member of the Soho Photo Gallery in Manhattan, she has won awards for her work. She often writes about the connections between psychology and photography and presented a paper on digital anxiety at the 2007 annual meeting of the American Psychological Association. Ruth has traveled extensively and, in addition to her digital portfolio of the Walking Dunes, she has photographed Anasazi ruins in the West, fish factory ruins along the Atlantic Coast, and old Jewish cemeteries in Germany.

Mike Bottini is a naturalist, writer and environmental consultant. After completing graduate studies in wildlife ecology at the University of British Columbia, Mike worked for fourteen years at the Group for the South Fork, a non-profit environmental advocacy organization. While there, he designed many of the trail systems in the region, including the two trails that traverse his favorite area: the Walking Dunes. He is an award-winning columnist, taught "Introduction to Environmental Science" at Southampton College and "The Nature of New York" at CUNY, and hosted WLIU's Nature News and Views weekly broadcast. Mike has done research on River Otters and Spotted Turtles, and he continues to introduce people to the natural world through his field naturalist classes, nature walks, and paddling trips. Mike has published two books: *Trail Guide to the South Fork* and *Exploring East End Waters: A Natural History and Paddling Guide.*

A Note on Photography

For many years I used the Nikon 6006 and the Olympus OM-1 with a macro lens, before switching to the medium-format Mamiya 6, all of them film cameras. In time I went digital, first to the point-and-shoot Nikon 8800, and then to the Nikon D80, a single lens reflex (SLR) camera. I find that I can be more productive in the field with a digital camera that doesn't run out of film at critical moments.

The main advantages of digital SLR cameras are their speed and convenience, not only in capturing wildlife, but also in ease of use, and in their immediate feedback. I use Adobe Photoshop CS3 to correct and improve what I've photographed.

My favorite time of day to photograph in the Dunes is late afternoon when the western sun bathes the landscape in rich golden, orange and red colors.

References

Attenborough, David. 1995. *The Private Life of Plants*. Princeton University Press, N.J.

Black, John A. 1993. The Napeague Dunes: Long Island, N.Y. The Proceedings of the Eighth Symposium on Coastal and Ocean Management. Vol. 2, New York: American Society Civil Engineers.

Bowman, Dwight D.1999. *Georgis' Parasitology for Veterinarians*. W.B. Saunders, Philadelphia, PA.

Camilleri, T. 1998. *Carnivorous Plants*. Simon and Schuster, Australia.

Davis, Dan and Mitchell Cangelosi. 2005. Field Trip to the Walking Dunes and Hither Hills. Department of Geosciences, Stony Brook University, N.Y.

Disreali, D. J. 1974. The Effect of Sand Deposits on the Growth and Morphology of Ammophila breviligulata. *Journal of Ecology* 72:1. pp. 145-154.

Englebright Steven C., Gilbert N. Hanson, Troy Rasbury, and Eric E. Lamont. 2000. *On The Origin of Parabolic Dunes Near Friar's Head, Long Island, New York*. Long Island Botanical Society Newsletter 10:1.

Fitzgerald, T. D. 1995. *The Tent Caterpillars*. Cornell University Press, Ithaca.

Fuller, Myron L. 1914. *The Geology of Long Island, New York*. U.S.G.S. Paper 82, Government Printing Office, Washington, D.C.

Johnson, Ann F. 1985. *Plant Communities of the Napeague Dunes*. Mad Printers, Mattituck, NY.

Johnson, Charles W. 1985. *Bogs of the Northeast*. University Press of New England, Hanover, NH.

Perry, Bill. 1985. *Sierra Club Naturalist's Guide: The Middle Atlantic Coast*. Sierra Club Books, San Francisco, CA.

Rice, Barry A., Ph.D.
FAQ — Author
http://www.sarracenia.com/faq.html
Galleria Carnivora — Curator
http://www.sarracenia.com/galleria/galleria.html
(personal communication)

Bill Cullina, "Rooted in Mystery-How Does the Pink Lady-slipper Grow?" *New England Wild Flower, Vol. 1, No. 1, Spring/Summer 1997*, page 1.

Bill Cullina, "Rooted in Mystery Part II-Growth Requirements of the Pink Lady-slipper," *New England Wild Flower, Vol. 1, No. 2, Fall/Winter 1997*, pp. 4-5.

Anne B. Wagner, "Pink Lady's Slipper Cypripedium acaule Fact Sheet," *North American Native Orchid Journal, Vol. 5, No.4*, pp. 317-324.

Schnell, Donald. E. 1976. *Carnivorous Plants of the United States and Canada*. Blair Publ., North Carolina.

Stefanik, J. 2004. Transplanting Pink Lady's-Slipper (*Cypripedium acaule*). New Hampshire Orchid Society.

Suffolk County Soil Survey. 1975. J. W. Warner et al. Soil Conservation Service, USDA.

Suffolk County Department of Public Works Five Town Topographical Maps

Taylor, Norman. 1923. *The Vegetation of Montauk: A Study of Grassland and Forest*. Brooklyn Botanic Garden, Brooklyn, N.Y.

Thien, L. B. & B. G. Marcks. 1972. The floral biology of Arethusa bulbosa, *Calopogon tuberosus* and *Pogonia ophioglossoides*. *Canadian Journal of Botany* 50:2319-2325.

Dubecky, Patricia E., Maher, Thomas J., 1994. A geomorphic analysis suggesting the origin of the migrating dunes at Napeague. First Conference on the Geology of Long Island and Metropolitan New York.

McKee, E.D., 1979. Introduction to a study of global sand seas. In: McKee, E.D., (editor). *A Study of Global Sand Seas*. United States Geological Survey, Professional Paper 1052. p. 3-19.